D0245615

SURVIVAL SKILLS HANDBOOK

DANGEROUS ANIMALS

Bear Grylls

This survival skills handbook has been specially put together to help young adventurers just like you to stay safe in the wild. Our planet is full of many wonderful and fascinating animals, but some of these animals come equipped with dangerous weapons. This book will teach you about some of the most dangerous animals on Earth, and how to keep yourself safe when you're out exploring the world.

Bear

CONTENTS

WHAT MAKES ANIMALS DANGEROUS?

When you are outdoors it's almost impossible to avoid meeting animals. Even if you walk down the street you are likely to meet several species including birds, insects, dogs, and cats within just a few metres of setting off.

Prepare

It is important to be prepared for problems with animals and to stay safe around them. Understanding animals and knowing what to do in an emergency is an important part of any adventure.

BEAR SAYS

The best way to stay safe around animals is to leave them undisturbed. Never approach even a pet dog without checking with the owner first if it is safe to do so.

Stay safe

Different animals have different features that can cause problems – even the smallest insect could be deadly, so don't assume that it is only large animals that can be dangerous.

Claws

Claws can be used to catch and hold prey, or just for digging, self-defence, or grooming. Cats have claws that can be hidden inside their paws to protect them from wear and tear when they aren't being used.

Teeth

Teeth are made of a different material to bones. Limpets have extremely hard teeth that are used to scrape algae from rocks.

Stings and venom

A sting is a sharp organ that pierces the skin of another animal and can inject venom – but not all stings are venomous. Most animals do not leave their stinger in the wound. Venom is a toxin that is designed to harm another animal.

WHY ANIMALS ATTACK

If you are going to stay safe it is important to understand why an animal might attack. Then you can avoid situations where a problem might occur.

Animal scent marking

Some animals urinate to mark out their territory. This is known as "scent marking". Other animals know to stay away when they smell this scent.

BEAR SAYS

Never get between a mother and her young, and keep well away from the babies. The instinct to protect the young is extremely strong.

Territory

Animals can also be extremely territorial. A territory is an area that an animal defends to hunt or forage. Be aware that if you enter their territory you may find yourself under attack until you leave.

It is extremely rare for an animal to attack a human because it is hungry. Most attacks are because the animal is surprised or frightened.

Fear

Nearly every species of animal experiences the emotion we know as fear. Most animals will run away if they feel frightened, but there are some situations where that doesn't happen and they might attack instead. An animal that is old, sick, or has babies may feel more threatened than usual – so keep away.

ARTHROPODS

These animals have an external skeleton, segmented bodies, and jointed limbs that are usually in pairs. This group of animals includes insects and crustaceans.

Mosquitoes

Mosquitoes are very small flies that consume the blood of other animals. The blood loss isn't usually a problem if you get bitten, but in some parts of the world the mosquito can carry nasty diseases, such as malaria and Zika virus, and may infect you when it decides to snack upon your blood.

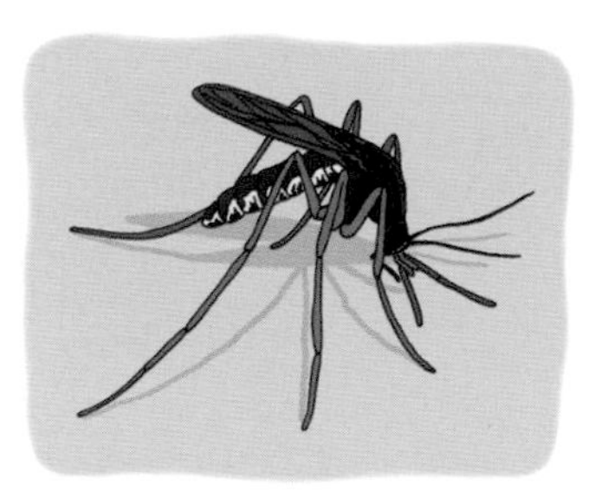

KEY

serious risk

minor risk

Distribution of malarial risk

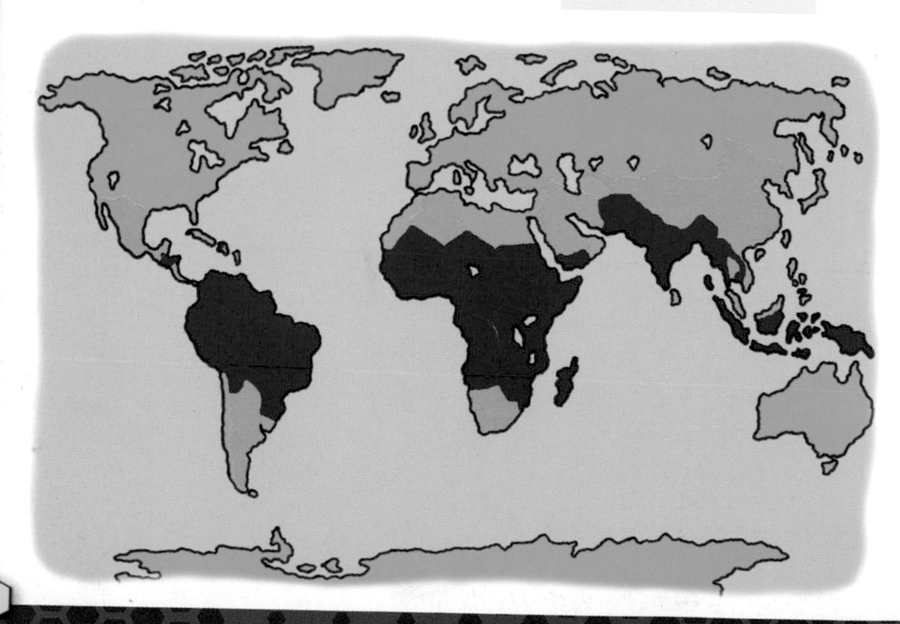

Anti-malaria advice

You cannot be vaccinated against malaria so it is important to take steps to protect yourself.

- Avoid mosquito bites.
- Be informed. Know exactly which areas are likely to be a problem and be aware that malarial mosquitoes typically bite after sunset and the risk often depends upon the time of year.
- Take anti-malarial tablets as directed by your doctor. Some types need to be taken weeks before you go on a trip, so be organised well in advance.
- Be aware of the symptoms of malaria.

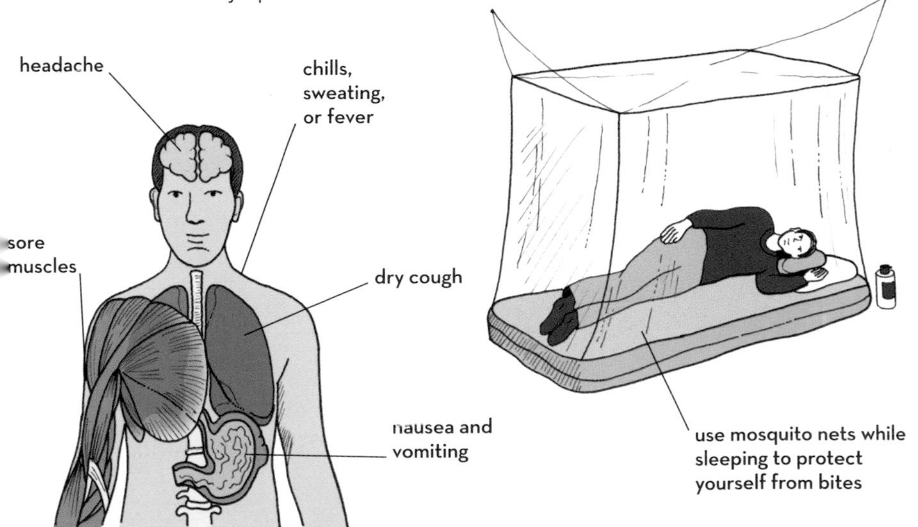

Survival tips

- If you think you have malaria, seek medical advice quickly, as it can be fatal.
- Malaria may not cause a concern for many months after your trip, so make sure you tell your doctor you have been to a malarial area if you are unwell even some time after you return.
- If you are going somewhere extremely remote you may be advised to carry emergency standby medication for malaria.

BEAR SAYS

It is important to see your doctor if you are planning to travel overseas to check if you are going to an area where malaria is common. You may be given anti-malaria medication to take.

Zika virus

This virus is mostly spread by a different mosquito to the type that carries malaria. These mosquitoes are most active during the day. Most people only suffer a very mild infection and they usually don't even notice they have it. However, Zika virus can cause serious birth defects if women are infected during pregnancy. Zika does not occur naturally in the UK, but any woman who is pregnant or trying to get pregnant needs to get medical advice before travelling to affected areas.

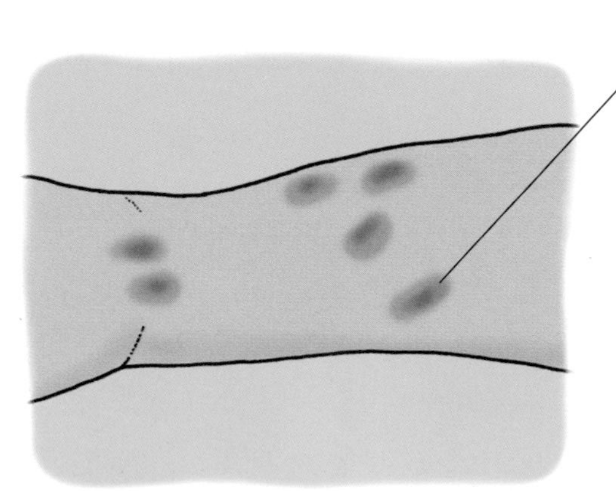

mosquito bites are normally red, itchy bumps

Dengue fever

Dengue fever is widespread in many parts of the world. Most people can fully recover within a week, but occasionally it can cause serious problems and even death. People in the UK can only catch dengue fever if they have recently travelled to a place where it is common. It is spread by a mosquito that bites near stagnant water mainly in the morning and early evening. Symptoms of dengue fever include a tummy ache and vomiting. Treatment is limited to painkillers, rest, and drinking plenty of water.

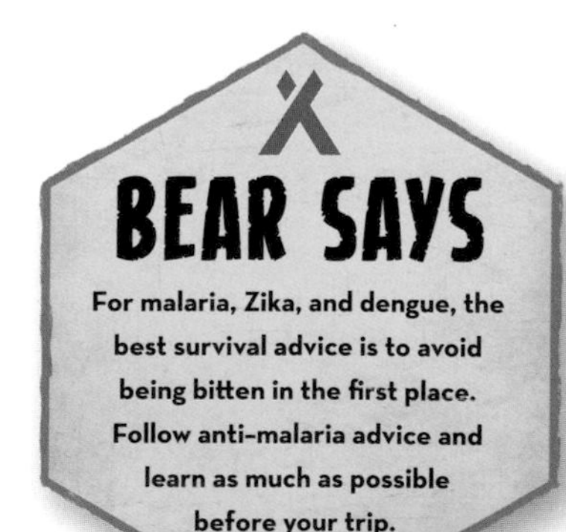

BEAR SAYS

For malaria, Zika, and dengue, the best survival advice is to avoid being bitten in the first place. Follow anti-malaria advice and learn as much as possible before your trip.

Dengue transmission

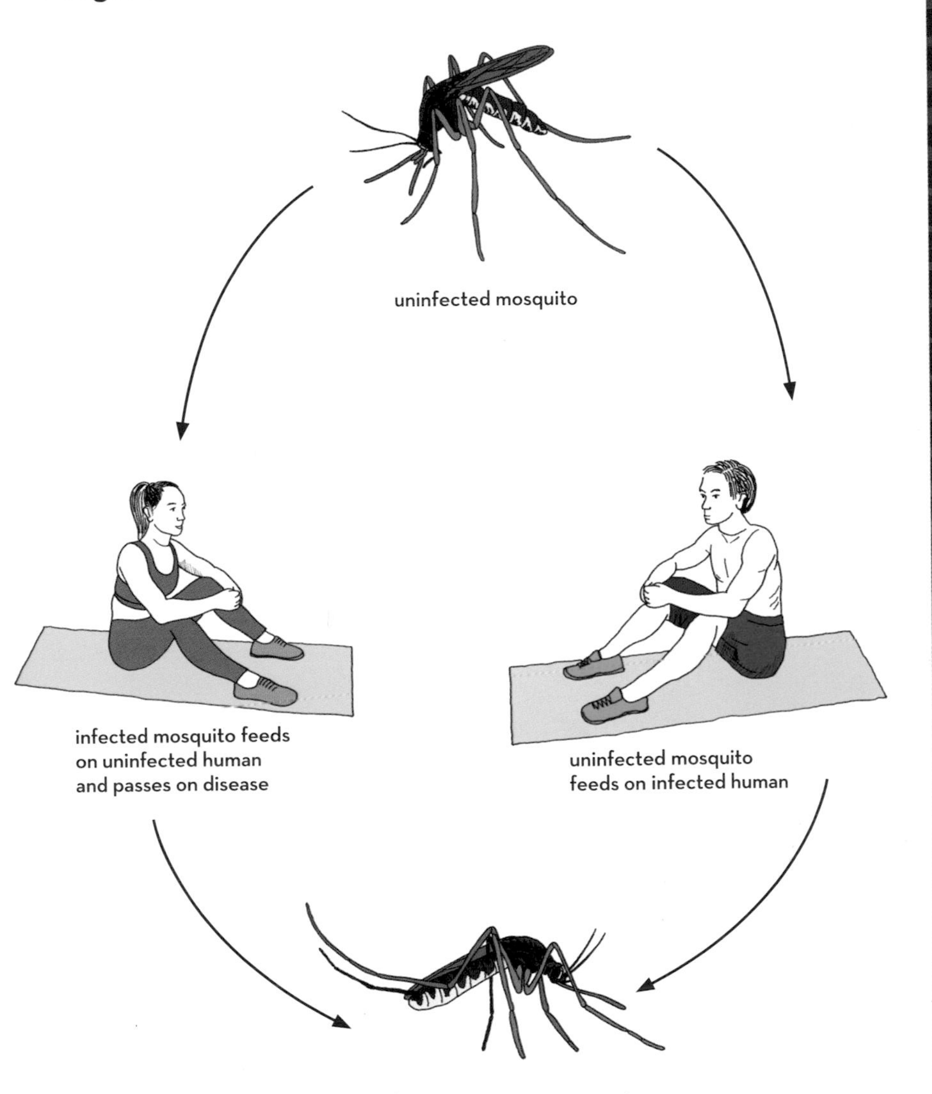

BEES, WASPS, AND HORNETS

Honey bees have barbed stingers that they cannot pull out of your skin after stinging, and so they then die. Most of the bees you see when out hiking are bumblebees and don't have barbed stingers.

Africanised honey bee

This bee is known as the "killer bee". It was deliberately introduced in Brazil to try to produce more honey, but some swarms escaped and it is now found in both South and North America.

barbed honey bee stinger

These bees have been known to chase a person for 50 m, so if you think you see one do not disturb it! They have killed humans.

distribution of Africanised honey bees

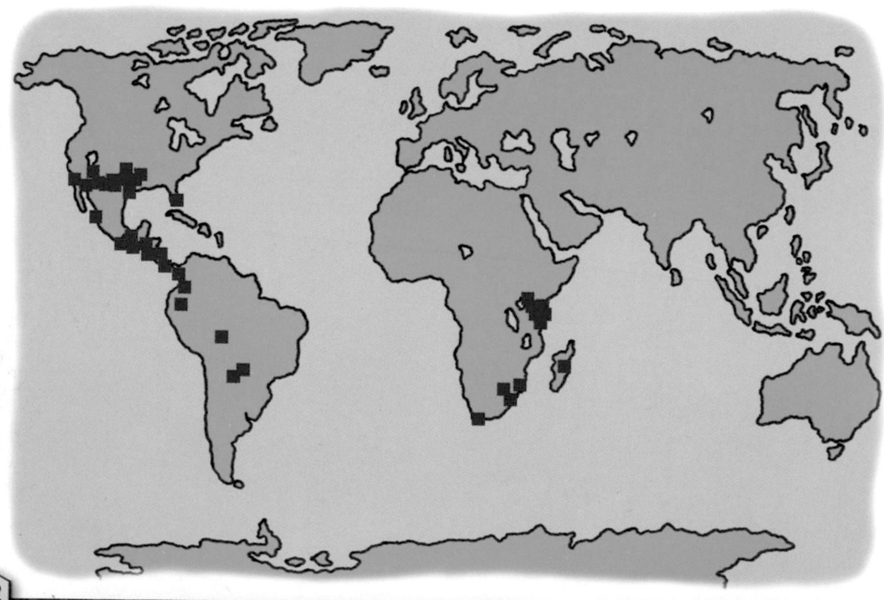

Survival tips

- Never disturb bees, wasps, or hornets.
- Don't wear perfume or bright colours, or eat and drink sugary foods nearby.
- Don't swat them or wave your arms around – stand still.
- Wear shoes and avoid loose clothing.
- Keep vehicle windows closed.
- If the sting is left in your skin, scrape it out with a bank card or similar using a sideways motion.
- Wash the area, elevate, and apply a cold compress.
- Painkillers may help. Avoid home remedies.
- Get medical help if you vomit, feel unwell, have been stung on the mouth, throat, or near the eyes, or if you have any swelling or breathing difficulties.

Wasps

Wasp stings may be painful but most people who get stung will get better in a few hours or days.

Hornets

Hornets are essentially large wasps, but the sting is more painful than a wasp sting because it injects more venom. Hornets and wasps can sting repeatedly as their stingers aren't barbed so they survive after stinging. The Asian giant hornet is thought to cause many deaths every year in Japan. It can set off an allergic reaction, multiple organ failure, and then the victims can die.

Always tell an adult if you've been stung, as some people can have a life-threatening allergic reaction.

SCORPIONS

A sting from a scorpion is painful but usually harmless. They glow when exposed to certain types of ultraviolet light. They use venom to kill or paralyse their prey and as defence against predators. Scorpions are found on all continents except Antarctica, but only very few species can kill a human.

Scorpion survival tips

- Wear long sleeves and gloves.
- Shake out clothes and shoes before putting them on.
- People with allergic reactions may need to carry an auto-injector pen (EpiPen®).
- If stung, apply a cold compress and use painkillers.
- Get medical attention if you feel unwell or have been stung by a dangerous species.

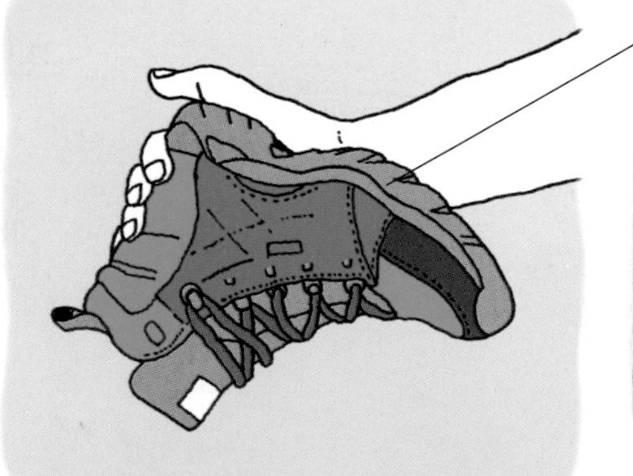

scorpions often shelter in dark places so always shake out boots before putting them on

BEAR SAYS

The fat-tailed scorpion is one of the most dangerous species in the world. It is found in the Middle East and Africa and kills several people each year.

SPIDERS

Spiders use their fangs to inject venom, but most species are harmless to humans.

Noble false widow spider

This is the UK's most venomous spider. It was relatively unheard of until recently – it was previously found just in the south of England, but its range has now increased. It looks similar to the notorious black widow spider. The noble false widow is believed to have first arrived in the UK in a crate of bananas from the Canary Islands.

Although a noble false widow's bite is painful, it is no more uncomfortable than a wasp sting and there have been no deaths reported in the UK.

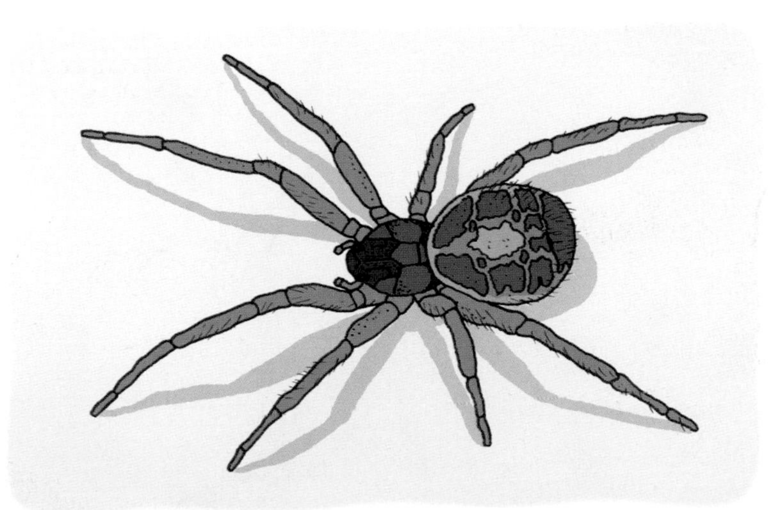

Brazilian wandering spider

Although this species is considered the world's most venomous spider, an effective antivenom exists and very few people die after being bitten. It's mainly found in tropical South America and its Greek name *Phoneutria* means "murderess".

Sydney funnel web spider

These venomous spiders are attracted to water and often fall into swimming pools. They can survive for several hours in the water and have been known to bite when removed from the pool. Luckily there haven't been any deaths since the appropriate first aid was understood and the antivenom was produced.

Treating a funnel web spider bite

Cover with a bandage. Get medical attention as soon as possible and do not remove the bandage.

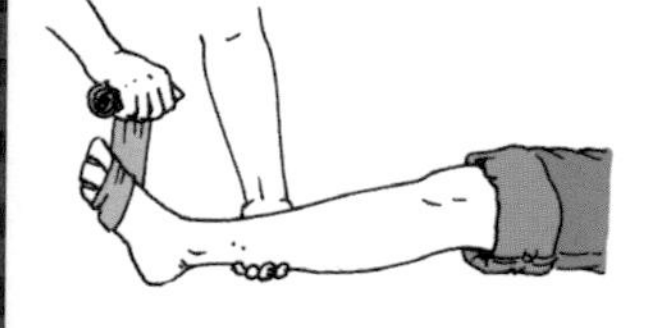

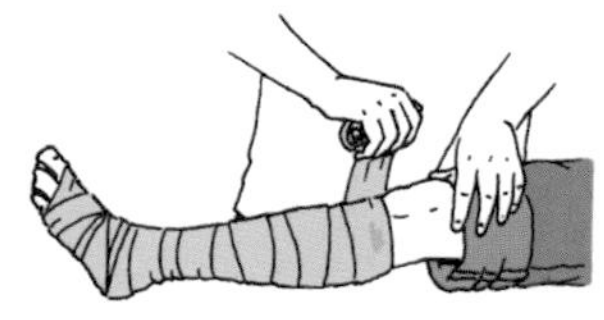

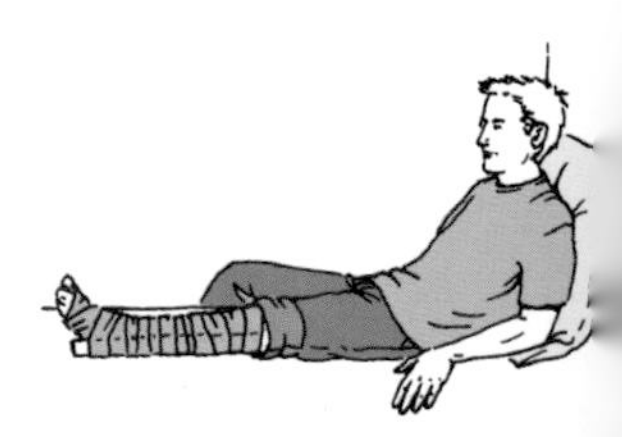

Redback spider

This mainly nocturnal spider can cause a problem because it likes living in people's houses. It mostly eats insects, and injects venom that turns the victim's innards to a liquid. A few minutes after injecting its prey, the spider sucks out the liquid. Many people are bitten every year by these spiders and the treatment ranges from taking painkillers, applying ice, and keeping still, to hospital care and antivenom if necessary. No deaths have been reported since 1956 when the antivenom was introduced.

FISH AND OTHER OCEAN LIFE

Most rivers and lakes contain very little salt compared to the sea – this is where you will find freshwater fish. Some fish spend time in both saltwater (the sea) and freshwater, or even prefer brackish water which is a mixture of saltwater and freshwater usually found in estuaries (where a river meets the sea).

Be prepared

If you are planning to go in or near the water during a trip, it is important to make sure you know about potential dangers in advance. Are there any dangerous fish or other marine life native to the area you are going to? Are there certain areas that are more dangerous or safe?

Warning signs

Often, if an area is known for dangerous fish or marine life, there will be danger signs posted to warn people to stay safe. If you see a purple flag, this is a sign that there is venomous or dangerous wildlife in the water. Red flags mean do not enter the water!

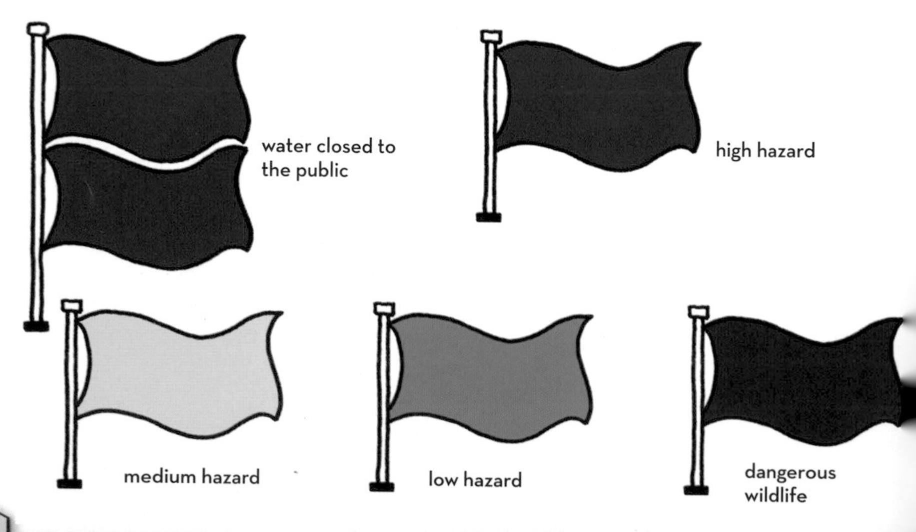

Water safety

Never go swimming alone, and always make sure there is a grown up nearby. Stay aware of your surroundings, and make sure you communicate with everyone you are with. Warn everyone if you think you spot anything that could be dangerous. It's always better to look a little silly than to risk somebody getting badly hurt.

If you think there is a chance that there is dangerous wildlife in the area, or are in any doubt, it's always safest to stay out of the water.

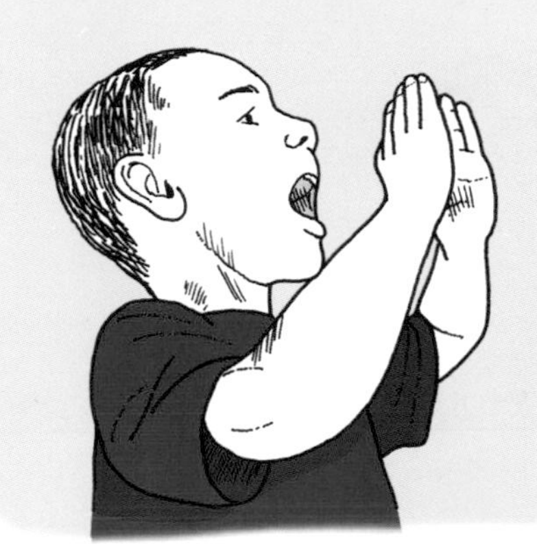

If someone is hurt

If someone begins to show signs of having been stung or bitten by a fish, get them out of the water immediately and call for help straight away. If you feel comfortable doing so, perform first aid on the victim. It might help to attend a first aid course before your trip.

Sharks and rays

There are more than 500 species of shark ranging in size from around 15 cm to 12 m long. They are found in all seas. They have between five and seven gills on each side of their heads and their side fins (pectoral fins) are not connected to their heads.

Great white shark

The great white is responsible for more human injuries and deaths than any other shark. Despite this, it actually prefers to eat other things. Great whites are famous for mistaking surfboards for seals, but they often break off contact after the first bite as they don't like the taste of humans and can't deal with all the bones! This habit is called a "test bite" and people die from blood loss rather than because the shark has eaten them.

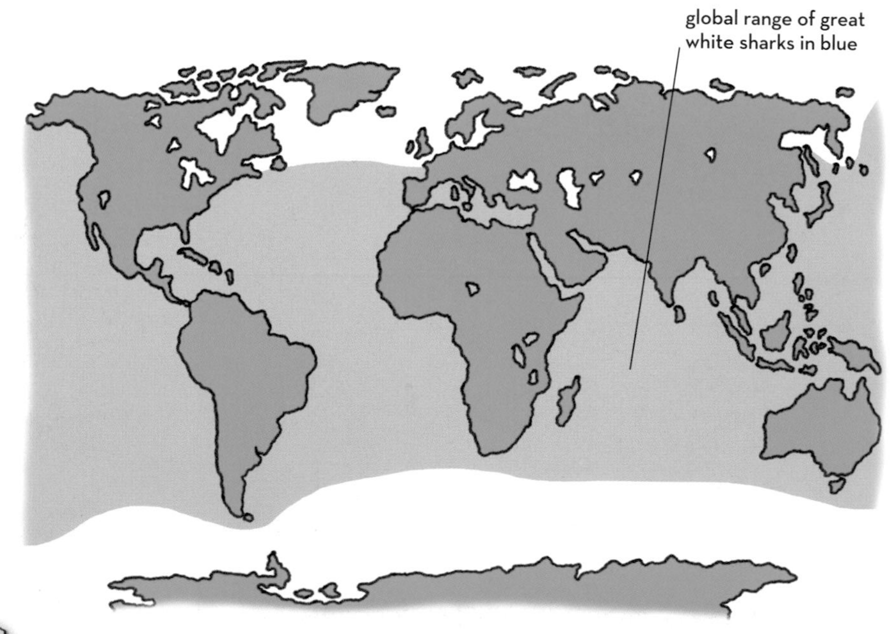

Rodney Fox

In 1963 he was severely injured by a great white when he was fishing and needed 462 stitches to repair the damage – it was a miracle that he survived at all. Since then he has spent more than 35 years fighting for shark protection laws – the great white is a protected species in Australia because of him.

Surviving a shark attack

- If you see a shark – leave it alone. Around half of attacks could have been avoided by not interfering with the fish.
- Try to remain calm, but get away from the place where a shark is attacking as fast as possible.
- Hit the shark in the eye or gills (not the nose) if you are trying to make it let go.
- Sharks can smell blood for over a mile so don't get in the water if you are bleeding and get out if you injure yourself.
- Avoid bright, flashy swimwear and jewellery as sharks are attracted to shiny things.
- Sharks often think that lots of splashing is an injured fish and can hear across very large distances.

Sting rays

These fish are related to sharks. They are mainly found in tropical and subtropical marine waters. Most rays have a venomous barbed stinger that is used for self-defence.

Steve Irwin

Steve Irwin was a television presenter and conservationist who was known for filming dangerous animals – particularly crocodiles. He was tragically killed in 2006 by a sting ray while filming as the barb went through his heart.

Odysseus

In Greek mythology Odysseus (the king of Ithaca) was killed by his son using a spear that had a sting ray barb on the point.

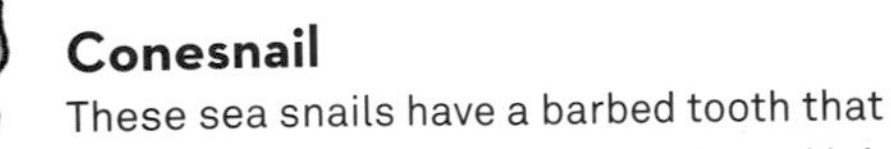

Conesnail

These sea snails have a barbed tooth that they can extend out of their heads and inject venom with. These larger tropical snails prey on small fish that live on the bottom of the ocean and can kill humans. They often have beautiful shells and people sometimes pick them up to look at them and get stung.

Stonefish

Considered one of the most venomous fish, stonefish are extremely well camouflaged and often sting people in Australia when they accidentally step on them – the foot pressing down causes a sharp spine to pop up. A sting can kill but is usually treated by putting the affected foot in hot water or administering antivenom in more serious cases. They can be eaten if the poisonous part is removed.

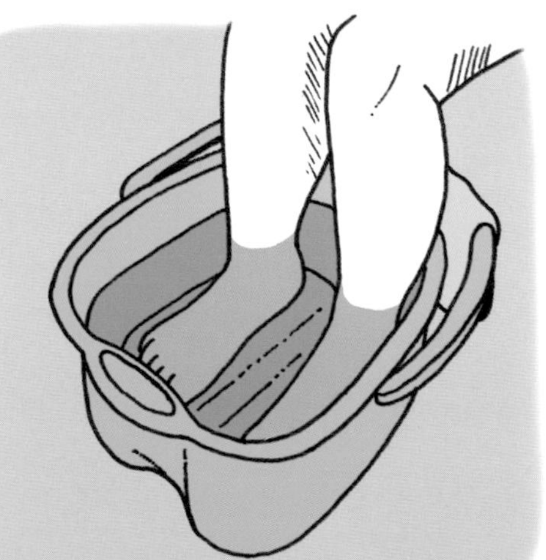

Blue ringed octopus

Octopuses are soft-bodied organisms with eight arms, or tentacles. Blue ringed octopuses are fairly small – around the size of a golf ball – and peaceful creatures if left alone. If disturbed these octopuses can bite, but the bite can be so small you may not even notice. However, each animal contains enough venom in its saliva to kill 26 adults within minutes and an antidote has not yet been invented.

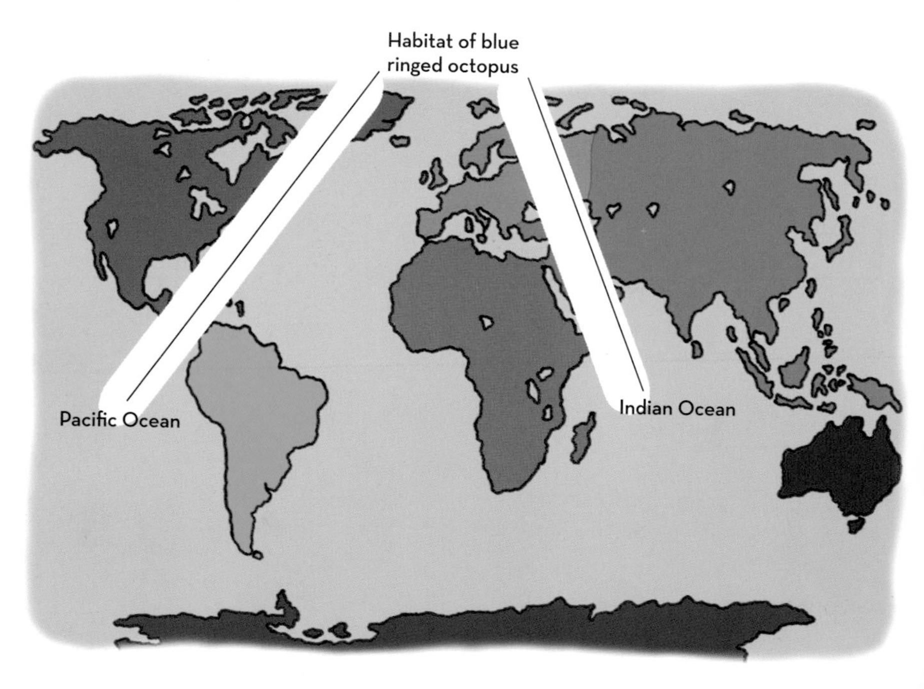

The blue rings flash as a warning when it is disturbed – it will flee as long as it isn't touched.

A 49 year old woman is reported to have been bitten on the leg by a blue ringed octopus when swimming off Stradbrooke Island, Australia. She was taken to hospital but didn't suffer any long term effects as it is thought that the octopus was unwell and somehow had less venom than usual.

BEAR SAYS

The blue ringed octopus kills by paralysing its victims so they cannot breathe. This eventually wears off so artificial respiration will save a life if it is continued until medical help arrives.

Jellyfish

These invertebrates are sometimes called "sea wasps" because their sting can be extremely painful. Some species have tentacles that are 3 m in length. Box jellyfish actively hunt for small fish, unlike all other jellyfish that just drift around waiting for food.

BEAR SAYS

It is important to find out how to swim safely in different areas of the world. Talk to people who know the area about what to look out for and, if in any doubt, stay out of the water.

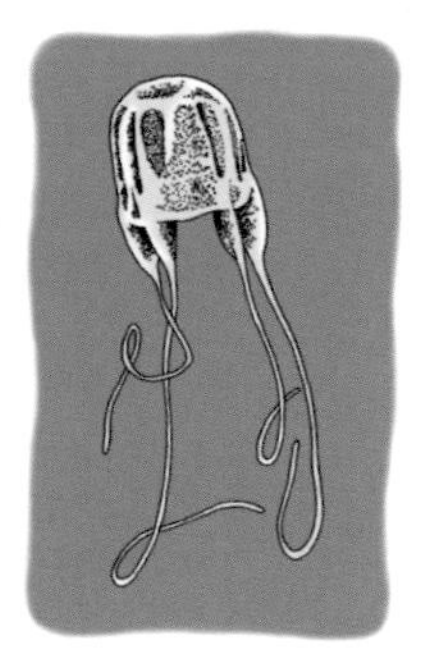

Box jellyfish

These jellyfish are almost transparent, and extremely difficult to see. Each tentacle has around 500,000 microscopic harpoons that fire venom into the prey.

KEY
- Chironex-style box jellyfish fatalities
- Irukandji-style box jellyfish fatalities
- Irukandji-style box jellyfish stings
- other jellyfish fatalities

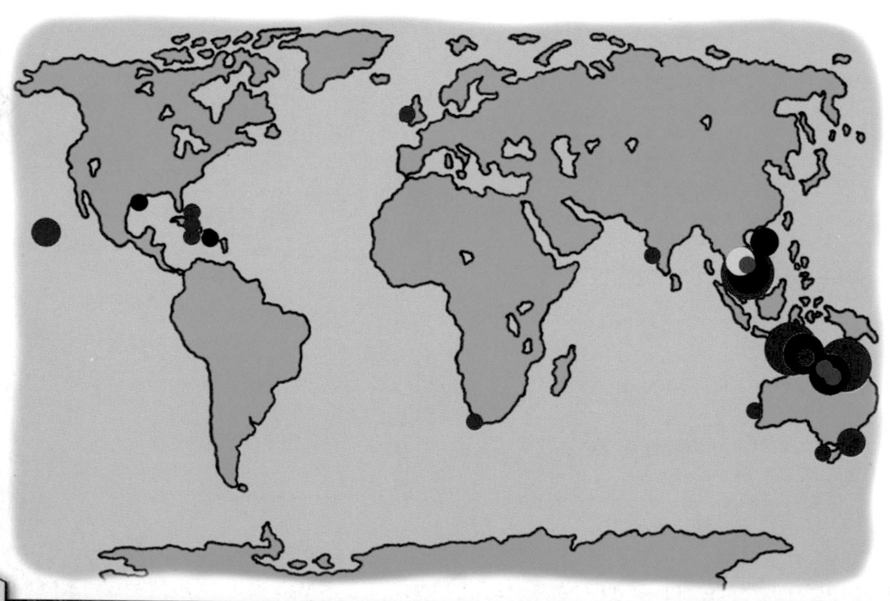

Many Australian beaches have vinegar in prominent places and nets placed around the bay in order to provide immediate first aid and protect swimmers. A German tourist was reported to have been killed and her friend injured by a box jellyfish when swimming at night in Koh Samui, Thailand in 2015. Jellyfish populations can dramatically increase during the wet season in this part of the world.

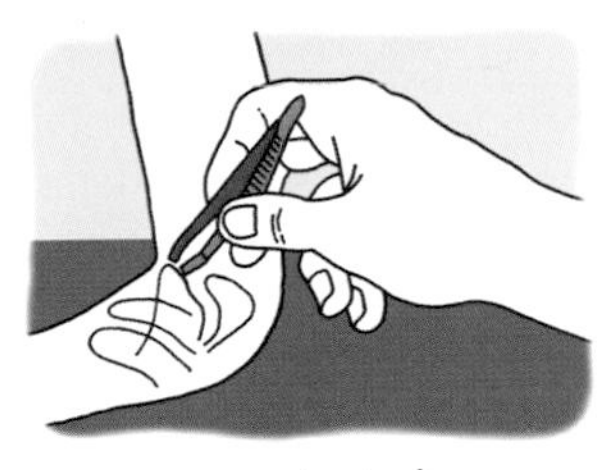

remove tentacles with tweezers

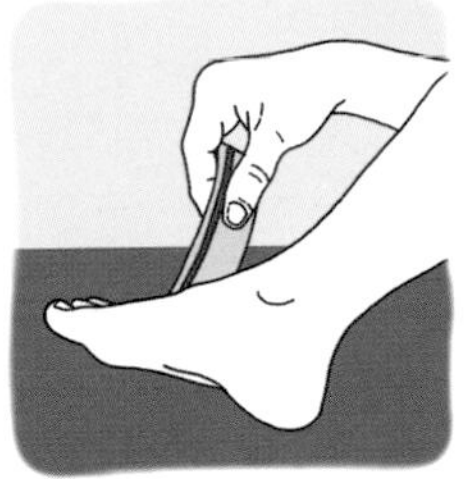

clean area

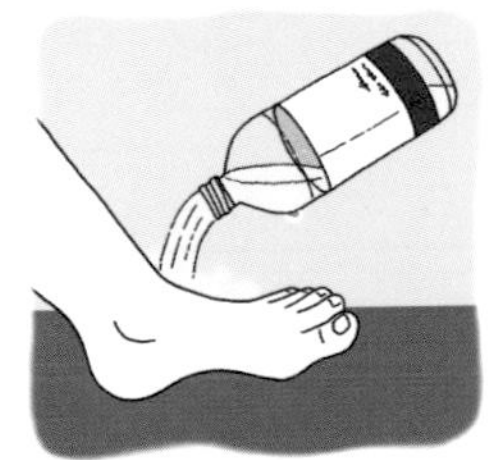

rinse with vinegar

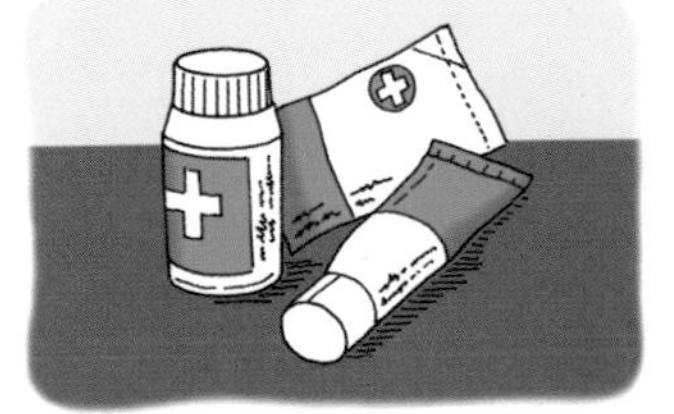

apply ice and take painkillers

Jellyfish sting survival guide

- Most jellyfish stings are mild and require simple treatment.
- Get the person out of the water.
- Remove any remaining tentacles using tweezers and wear gloves if possible.
- Apply a heat pack or put the affected area in hot water.
- Painkillers may help.
- f they have difficulty breathing or have been stung in the face or the genitals call for medical help.
- Vinegar has been shown to stop the box jellyfish from continuing to discharge its stingers – urinating on the sting is said to be unlikely to help.

Pufferfish

These fish are mostly found in the tropics – never in cold waters. There are lots of species of pufferfish. They are usually slow, but can put on a sudden burst of speed when frightened. This is their primary defence against predators.

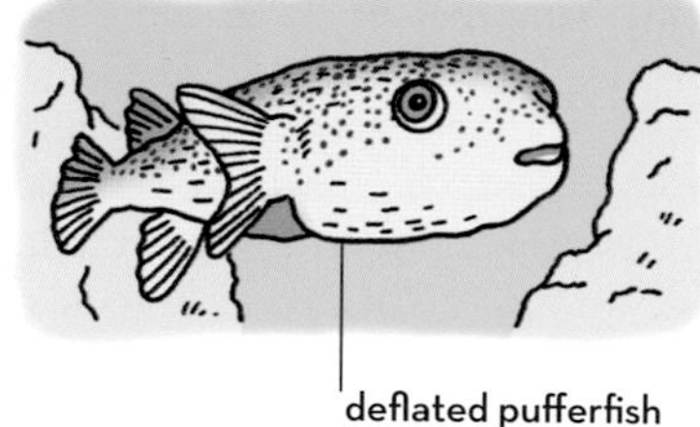

Secondary defence

They also have an extremely elastic stomach, which fills with water (or air if taken out of water) and spiny, often poisonous skin and internal organs. This secondary defence mechanism is designed to choke and poison a predator if they get swallowed. Not all species of pufferfish are toxic.

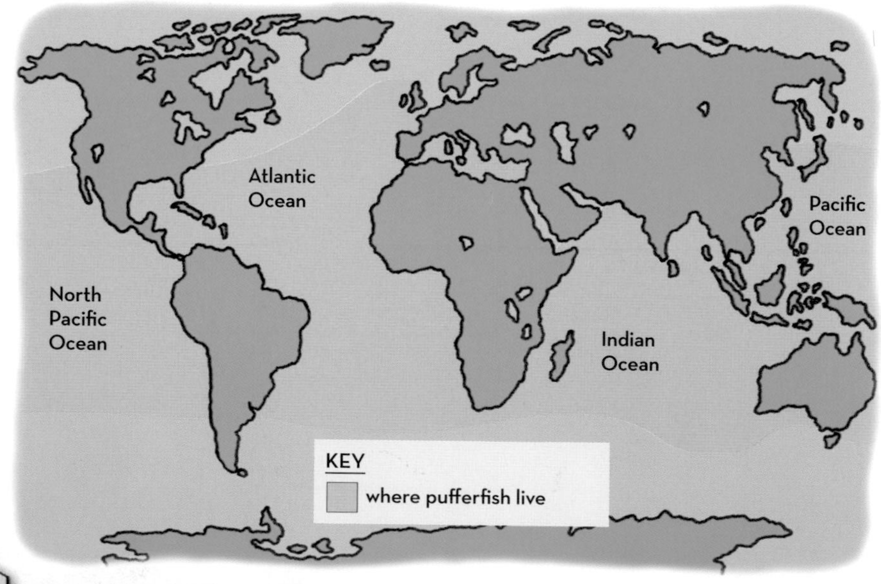

Fugu

Despite being highly toxic, some species of pufferfish are considered a delicacy in Japan. The fish is prepared by highly trained chefs who cut away the toxic parts. To be a fugu chef takes years of training and a difficult test as people could die if mistakes are made. A Japanese restaurant was closed for five days in 2015 after some customers were unwell after eating fugu. It is reported that they asked to eat the liver, which is regarded as a toxic material. The liver contains a toxin 100 times more lethal than cyanide.

REPTILES AND AMPHIBIANS

Reptiles have scaly skin and cold blood, and live mostly in hot places to warm up their bodies. While reptiles live on dry land, amphibians have adapted to survive in both water and land.

Lizards

There are over 6,000 different species of lizards, ranging from tiny chameleons the size of your thumbnail to giant lizards bigger than a human.

Komodo dragon

This is a lizard found on some of the Indonesian Islands. It is a large lizard that can grow up to 3 m long – that's longer than a human is tall. It tastes and smells with its tongue.

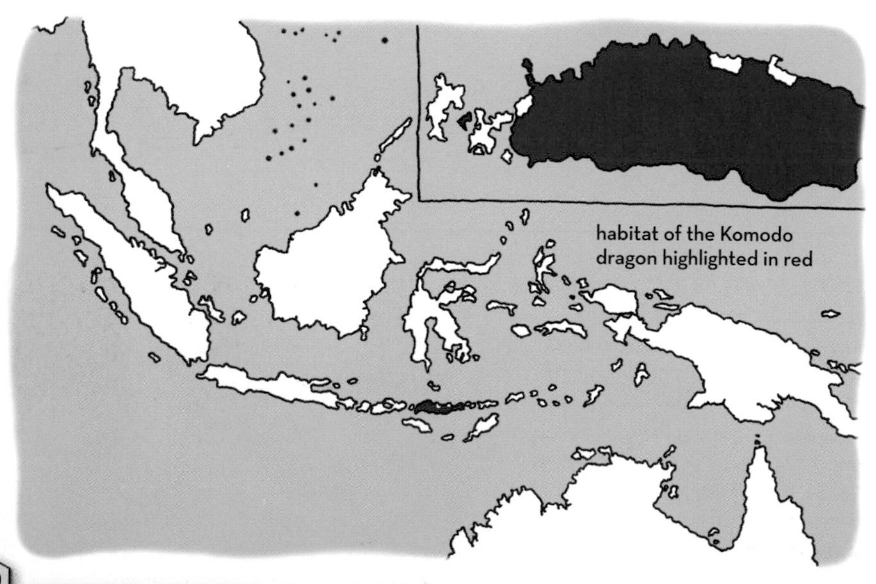

Venomous bite

Komodo dragons have a venomous bite and the poison released stops blood from clotting. They eat mainly decaying deer flesh (known as carrion). They can eat up to 80 percent of their own body weight per meal, but may only need to eat around 12 meals per year. People used to think that their saliva had special harmful bacteria in it so that a lick could kill, but it has recently been discovered that their saliva is the same as that of any other carnivore. Instead, it has venom produced in two glands near its mouth which is released when it bites.

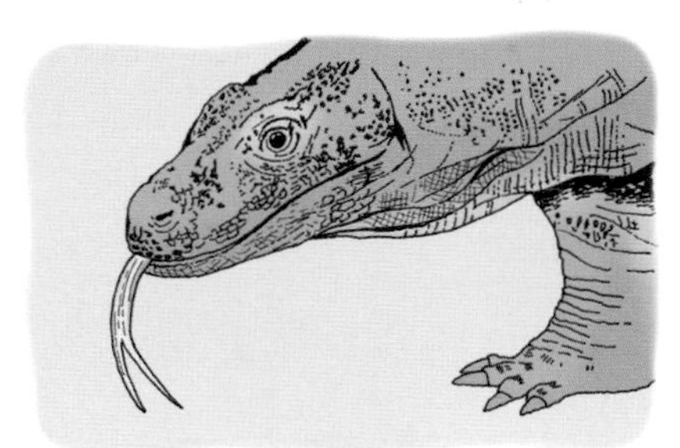

Danger to humans

Although attacks on humans are rare, a hungry komodo would attempt to catch and eat a human.

size of a Komodo dragon compared to an adult man

Komodo dragon survival story

In 2008 three British divers lost their boat in bad currents in Indonesia and were very glad to be washed up on an island, safely out of the shark infested water. Their happiness was short-lived, though, as a komodo dragon spotted them and only retreated when they threw stones at it. They ate shellfish until they were rescued after two sleepless nights on the island.

Poison dart frog

The most poisonous species in this frog family tend to be the most brightly coloured – which is useful as a warning not to eat them. They are considered some of the most brilliantly coloured animals on Earth. They are only a few centimetres long and are diurnal (active during the day). They are found in Central and South America and eat ants, mites, and termites, and it is their diet that makes them poisonous.

blue poison dart frog

A 5 cm long poison dart frog has enough poison to kill 10 adults. Scientists are currently studying these chemicals in the hope of making new medicines.

male frog carrying eggs on his back

Male poison dart frogs are known for their extremely good parenting skills – they carry eggs and tadpoles on their backs, and often bring up their young on their own.

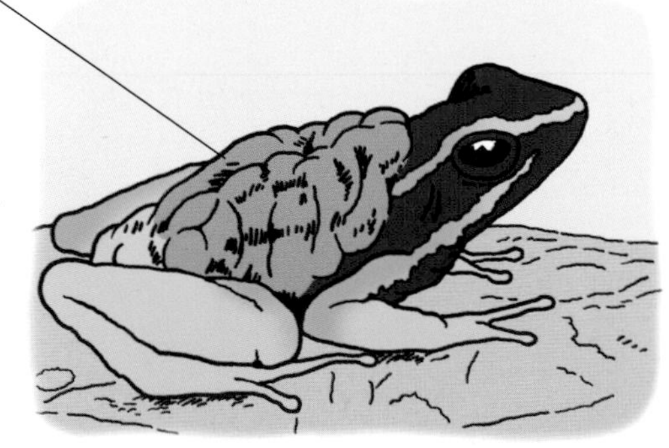

If a poison dart frog is raised in captivity and fed a diet that doesn't include insects, then it isn't poisonous.

Hunting

Hunters from Colombia's Embera tribe used the toxin from the poison dart frog to make poison arrows which were then fired at prey and helped to kill them quickly. This practice may have died out recently.

Crocodiles and alligators

What's the difference?

Alligator

- Wide, rounded snout
- Stronger
- Darker skin
- Eats turtles
- Can grow to 3.4 m long
- Lower teeth are hidden when mouth is shut
- Webbed feet
- Can live for 30–50 years
- Found in U.S. and China
- Live in fresh or brackish water – can't tolerate salt water
- Less aggressive

Crocodile

- Thin, pointed snout
- Weaker
- Lighter skin
- Eats fish and mammals
- Can grow to 5.8 m long
- Some lower teeth visible when mouth is shut
- Feet not webbed
- Can live for 70–100 years
- Found in U.S., Africa, Asia, Australia, and the Americas
- Can tolerate salt water
- More aggressive

BEAR SAYS

Alligators and crocodiles are said to be particularly attracted to dogs. Keep dogs away from the water and on leads.

Crocodile attack

A young woman was bitten by a crocodile in Western Australia in 2012 and survived. She was paddling in a freshwater pool when the crocodile grabbed her by her leg and pulled her underwater – crocodiles do this to try to drown their prey. Two people jumped in to save her and the crocodile let go when one of them dug his thumbs into the crocodile's eyes. Surgeons battled for four hours to save her leg and the people that came to her rescue were given bravery awards.

Alligator attack

A man and his seven-year-old son were swimming in a park in Florida when an alligator attacked the father and clamped its mouth around his head. The man reached up and pulled the jaws apart with all his strength and eventually it let go. He needed 50 stitches and staples but recovered.

How to survive a crocodile or alligator attack

- Learn where they live and stay away – be vigilant.
- At dusk or night they are most dangerous – use a torch and look for eye shine.
- Don't provoke or feed them.
- Keep children supervised and away from the edge of the water.
- Set up camp well above the high tide line.
- Keep food in a secure place.
- If you are in the water when you see one, swim to shore, splashing as little as possible.
- If you are charged by a crocodile or an alligator run away in a straight line – you should just about be able to outrun it.
- If one is biting you and won't let go – aim for the eyes and head and fight hard.
- If you are dragged underwater try to hit it below the tongue as there is a valve there that keeps water out – if you can hit this it should let go.
- Call for immediate help and get all wounds checked as even a minor wound can get infected from the bacteria in their mouths.

Snakes

There are more than 3000 species of snake – they live in every continent except Antarctica. Only around 725 species are venomous and of these only around 250 are able to kill a human with a single bite. Most non venomous snakes kill their prey by either swallowing them alive or by constriction (squeezing them).

Snake safety

- Look out for warning notices.
- Wear boots and long trousers.
- Never pick up a snake – even if you think it is dead.
- Use a stick instead of your hands to get things out of holes.
- If you see a snake, stand still. They will then usually move away from you.
- Learn about the different types of snake in areas where you are travelling.

Snake bite protection

- Keep calm and stay with the person that has been bitten.
- Remember the shape, size, and colour of the snake (take a photo if this is safe).
- Remove jewellery from the affected limb in case it swells up.
- Keep the area that has been bitten as still as possible to prevent the venom spreading around the body as much as possible.
- Call for medical help.

Cleopatra and the asp

Cleopatra was an Egyptian ruler. She is said to have killed herself by encouraging a venomous snake to bite her after her husband killed himself. Sadly, the husband had only done this because he falsely thought that Cleopatra had killed herself first. This myth is so famous that even Shakespeare wrote about it.

Carpet viper

These snakes are most active after dark. They rub their bodies together to produce a sizzling sound that is a warning. They are mainly found in Africa and India and are extremely well camouflaged so people get bitten as they accidentally disturb them. They often die before medical help arrives.

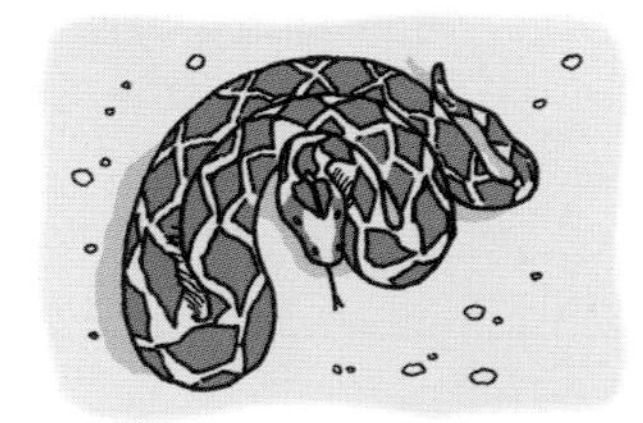

Black mamba

In 2013, a 13-year-old boy in Kenya was bitten by a black mamba. He arrived in hospital in a bad way, around 90 minutes after being bitten. He received antivenom medicine and was improving after two hours of treatment. By the next day he was able to go home.

Boa constrictor

Boa constrictors have no venom but they can still give a very painful bite if they are threatened. They will hiss as a warning and then squeeze their prey to suffocate it. They then eat their prey whole and can take weeks to digest it.

MAMMALS

Mammals are warm-blooded animals covered in hair or fur. They are incredibly versatile and exist on every continent. Many mammals are harmless, but many are deadly predators.

Hippopotamus

This highly aggressive and unpredictable mammal is considered one of the most dangerous animals in Africa. They are frequently reported to have attacked boats.

BEAR SAYS

David Livingstone is famous for having been attacked by a lion and putting the broken bones back in place himself with no pain relief – ouch!

David Livingstone

David Livingstone (1813–1873) was a Scottish explorer, doctor, and missionary who was obsessed with finding the source of the River Nile. On the Orange River in Africa his boat was attacked by an angry hippo, though luckily he and his crew survived.

Platypus

This is an egg-laying mammal (mammals don't usually lay eggs) that is found in Australia. When it was first discovered, scientists thought somebody was playing a joke on them because it has so many unusual features. The male platypus has a spur (claw on the back of the foot) on its hind foot that can cause a lot of pain if it kicks a human. It's such a special animal that the Australians have a picture of it on one of their coins.

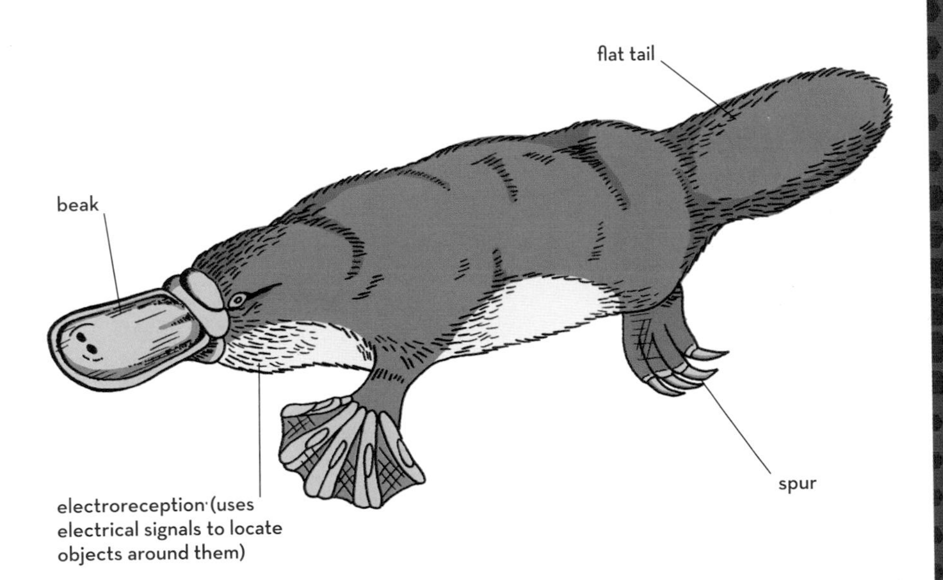

BIRDS

Birds live on all seven continents, and range from tiny hummingbirds to huge flightless birds like the ostrich. Birds who hunt other animals for food are called birds of prey, or raptors.

Cassowary

This large flightless bird is found in Australia. It is aggressive, unpredictable, has claws like daggers, and can break bones with a kick. They are great runners and have been known to chase people for miles. Hiding up a tree or playing dead have been reported as ways to survive – but they can wait around for ages!

BEAR SAYS

Birds don't make or inject venom, but they can become poisonous if they eat certain other poisonous creatures.

Ostrich

Like the cassowary, these flightless birds are unpredictable and can outrun a human. The American singer Johnny Cash was attacked by an ostrich he owned in 1981 and suffered broken ribs and an abdominal injury. He managed to fight it off with a stick.

Canada goose

Stay away from their nests and young or they may chase or even bite you.

Seagull

These birds have been known to attack if they think their chicks are in any danger. They give a warning call, a low pass over, then vomit or poo on you. Then they can swoop down and peck at your head, sometimes drawing blood!

Blue capped ifrita

This bird eats a certain kind of beetle that gives it a self-defence mechanism. The bird becomes poisonous to handle and can cause numbness and tingling if gloves aren't worn. It is found in the rainforests of New Guinea.

Pitohui

In Papua New Guinea this is known as the "rubbish bird" because the skin and feathers are poisonous if eaten.

VENOM AS MEDICINE

Although venom is dangerous and may even be deadly, it can also be very useful to humans. Doctors and scientists have found many different uses for animal venom, including medicines, painkillers, and vaccinations, and can even use the venom of one animal to treat a bite or sting from another.

Painkillers

Strong painkillers that might be given to someone with a bad injury can have nasty side effects including addiction. Scientists have been studying the venom from Chinese centipedes in order to develop medicines that can help with pain in humans without these unwanted side effects. Early results of their trials look very promising but it will be several years before the testing is fully finished. Venom from cone snails and black mamba snakes has also produced results that look useful.

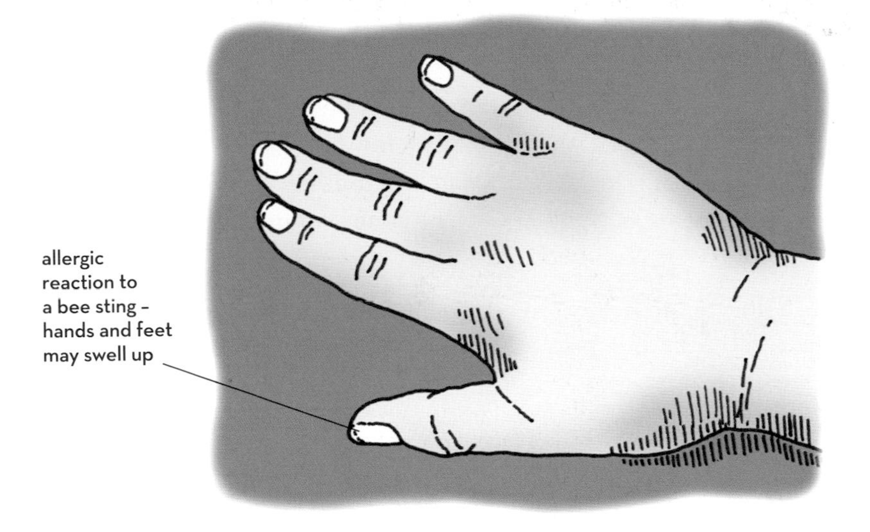

Sting allergies

Some people have an allergy to bee or wasp stings that can be life threatening. If doctors feel that it would be useful, they can offer a treatment called desensitisation. The patient is regularly injected with diluted bee or wasp venom for several years. This can be very useful in preventing a really bad reaction but has to be done very carefully in hospital in case the person becomes unwell.

These treatments, while very helpful, should only be administered by a doctor or nurse. If you are stung or hurt, seek medical help.

Cancer treatment

A doctor has developed a paint from scorpions that glows and attaches itself to brain tumour tissue. This helps surgeons to see the tumour and be sure that they have removed all the cancerous tissue when they perform operations.

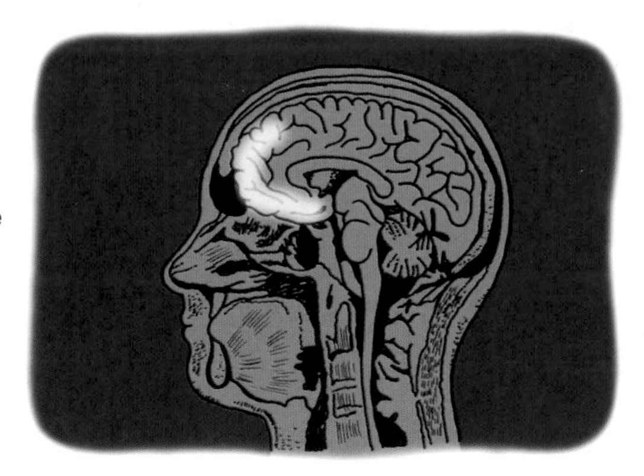

Heart attacks

Some snake venom contains a chemical that can stop blood clots from forming. A heart attack can occur when a blood clot blocks a blood vessel in the body. Medicines that contain venom are already used to prevent or treat minor heart attacks. More research is continuing in order to help more people with heart failure, and snake venom may also be used to treat other problems such as cancer.

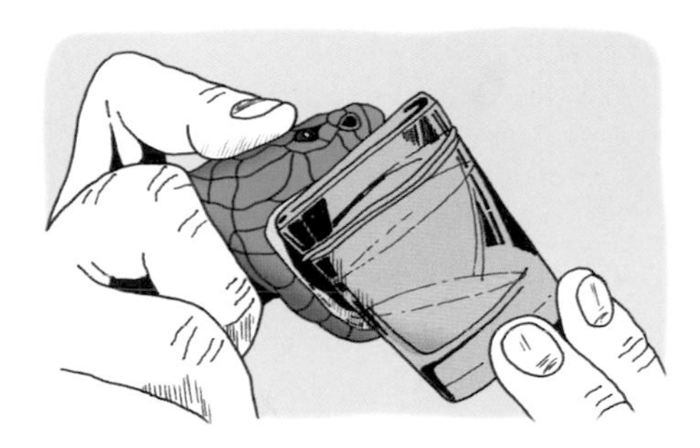

GLOSSARY

Algae – simple plants that can be tiny.

Antivenom – a medicine used to treat bites from venomous animals. Usually there is a specific antivenom for each animal.

Conservationist – a person who protects wildlife and the environment.

Continent – a very large land mass on Earth.

Crustacean – animals that have segmented bodies and two-part limbs. They usually live in water.

Cyanide – a chemical containing carbon and nitrogen. It is usually toxic.

Diurnal – active during the daytime rather than at night.

External – outside.

Fatal – deadly.

Incubation – the time between catching an infection and the symptoms appearing, when the infection develops.

Infect – to contaminate.

Instinct – a pattern of behaviour that an animal is born with.

Invertebrate – an animal without a backbone.

Missionary – a person sent to an area to carry out religious work.

Myth – a traditional story.

Nocturnal – an animal that is active during the night and sleeps during the day.

Predator – an organism that exists by preying on something else.

Segmented – divided into parts.

Stagnant – water or air that isn't flowing.

Territory – an area of land.

Toxin – a poisonous substance produced within a living thing.

Transparent – see-through or clear.

Vaccinate – give someone a special chemical that prevents them from getting a particular disease.

Patients' Rights, Law and Ethics for Nurses